Greenfields

RICHARD PRICE was born in 1966 and grew up in Scotland. He trained as a journalist at Napier College, Edinburgh, before studying English and Librarianship at the University of Strathclyde, Glasgow. *Lucky Day* (Carcanet 2004), a Book of the Year in *The Guardian* and in *Scotland on Sunday*, was shortlisted for several prizes, including the Whitbread. He has two children and lives in London, where he is Head of Modern British Collections at the British Library.

T0167440

Also by Richard Price from Carcanet

Lucky Day

RICHARD PRICE

Greenfields

CARCANET

Acknowledgements

I am especially grateful to the following editors who first published versions of several of the component sequences in this book: Ian and Sally King of Diehard Poetry (*Frosted, Melted*), Hamish Whyte of Mariscat Press (*Renfrewshire in Old Photographs*), Raymond Friel of Southfields Press (*Tube Shelter Perspective*), and Leona Medlin of Vennel Press (*Sense and A Minor Fever*). Other poems here were first published in *Chapman, New Review of Literature, Markings* and *PN Review*. 'Open the paper window' was written for a Christmas visit to Budapest under the auspices of the Scottish Poetry Library and *Parnasszus* magazine. Thank you especially to Dorothy Stirling who has again allowed the use of one of her beautiful paintings for the cover of my book.

For Donny O'Rourke and for my family

First published in Great Britain in 2007 by
Carcanet Press Limited
Alliance House
Cross Street
Manchester M2 7AQ

A CIP catalogue record for this book is available from the British Library
ISBN 978 1 85754 920 1

The publisher acknowledges financial assistance from Arts Council England

Typeset by XL Publishing Services, Tiverton
Printed and bound in England by SRP Ltd, Exeter

Contents

The milk-money round   1

Frosted, Melted
Hinges   5
15 and a jar of instant   7
Compressor   8
Joiner   9
With reverse   10
Translation   11
Wood raspberries   12
Hydro Hotel   13
Glinchy   14
Elan   15
The Kirstys   16
Nick in the isotherm   17
My father's record collection   18

Renfrewshire in Old Photographs
Reservoir   21
Facts about trout   22
In spate   23
In the Parish of St Fillan   24
Dash   25
Crash   26
Dry bed   27
Hillman Avenger   28
John Gallagher   29
Ghosts, Craigends House   30
Inscription for the Manor Pool   31
Deb to deb   32
Inscription for the Laverock Stone   33
Fifteen years   34

Quilted Leather
The Argument   37
Piecing   38
Describe me inaccurately I said   40
Covering   42
Scraps   43

Gentians

The day before my mother's funeral	47
My mother's palette	48
Difficult sky	49
At ease	50
The last kitchen	51

Tube Shelter Perspective 55

Foals of the Foals

With is	83
Stopper	84
Saying the swim	85
Taking hand	86
The wedding rings	87
At length	88
Sense and a minor fever	89
Doodlebug	90
Singer	91
Foals of the foals	92
The battle of the horses	93
At a Mary	94
Love charm of Cong, Co. Mayo	96

The Giant

The Giant	99
Texts	102
When the animals are freed	103
A traditional activity	104
Small dense hours	105

Duchal Wood 109

Open the paper window 113

The milk-money round

The smell of roadworks has struck bone
in my memory: a pipeline shows.
The pungent yellow air is broom
and tarmac and Jubilee rose.

This writing is a milkman's boy
treading gravel, pressing blind bells —
collecting change, pausing.
Seeking… intimate halls.

Frosted, Melted

Hinges

On the airstrip: fog.
Nothing taking off.
Five in the afternoon,
more or less.

I'd have called it a 'flitting'
but it was a year before I was born –
to my father it was 'moving house'.
He was Ma's envoy in Scotland:
he'd just chosen a field
that would grow into a bungalow
and he'd pay for it
when the bathroom,
opening on the hall
with a frosted glass door,
trapped her, towelnaked,
before the postman
and something to be signed for.

Through the same melted glass
I saw my first memory:
my eldest brother, nine or ten,
was stretching and not touching anything,
petrolburns on his face and hands,
a human X at the front door
(on a building site a friend
had clicked him alight;
we still don't know the bet).

On the airstrip: fog, night.
Eleven o'clock.
My father is being practical
on the hotel phone:
'I am speaking
back in my room.'

In the morning in England,
like a new couple
two police officers stood back
as Ma opened the door.
They had to be reassured:
she gave them tea in the fine bone.

(Just beyond the wicker of radar
the first plane out, just past midnight,
had dropped like a figurine.)

In the afternoon
my mother met my father in Arrivals.
Before they held held held each other
he says 'We just shook hands.'

15 and a jar of instant

There'll be no thirteens on this estate

so here's a baker's dozen, plus one, plus one:
lawn proud and redchip, horseshoe and geraniums.

We are talking Great Universal,
Avon and *denier*. This is yoghurt, vinyl,
the age of the wagon prams.

(A third boy's five fivestones,
sill-high on the outside
glimpse a jar of instant –
fall back, smack
into his hand,
the winning catch.)

There'll be no thirteens on this estate,
so here's a baker's dozen – plus one,
plus one.

Compressor

A mash of half-bricks, offcuts of board, glaur.
The first foam of alyssum.

Bungalows crating up the fields. Skelfy yellow rafters
dreeping girls. Finished halls.

A manhole lid, a lazy boy. A bath of petrol, a
cigarette's disfigurement, teenage inferno.

Twenty years later: a carpenter, a father, a face saved.

Joiner

A lounge with coal-dust on its lip:

December and my grandfather
is a joiner –
beech bricks on the floor's field.

The shock is the light
sucked from the Tree
(I think of me – as just teeth).

Mum is religious, and I
have tasted volts.

With reverse

Flames' makings,
newspapers.

The neatness
of folding words,
of folding men in suits,
men in shorts,
men.

Coal is a rock that burns
but sand will not burn.

And my fingers, dry,
grey, aching,

literate ash.

Translation

The stream runkles its sheet over the pebbles we've just skimmed. My hands are paws. Yours have an arthritis now as if you've been stroking cats all your life.

Our clothes are clothes your mother'd call tinker's dirt, my trainers clogs of mud, maquettes of feet.

In the flashback of water you are just trembling but you're a boulder to me, a father's stride safekeeping the depths, baptising the weakest child, the air hazy, like scentless petrolfumes singeing your tree-green anorak (heat of a May morning, its practical joke). The stream is a ritual dish, less than lukewarm, a game among boys, two boys in their own circumference, and brown trout maybe tickling my shins, wanting to gut me, nudging. And I'm splashing, shoving you to make you stagger in your waders, like a man shackled by his own jeans – round his ankles – like a little boy too young to wear long trousers.

(In the quiet, in the shelter of the bank, on a rock, two folk incapable of work – skimming stones.)

Wood raspberries

White leaves because you had to look up.
Smoother seen.
Green now, coarse side understood.
Yellow berries
(reds easy as blisters).
'Don't say thanks, taste the yellows.'
'Forget the cigarettes.'
Foxes slept here maybe.
A waspbeehornet stung an ear –
a tangerine shirt and lip-salve caused it.

Hydro Hotel

The derelict hotel, the tower on the hill,
water in the tower,
the height of the tower, the place I...

The stairways can't be trusted,
the lintels are arch.

The boy at lie
knows the balance of the woodpigeon,
the balance of his brothers,
my brothers, myself up here.

Brown light-switches and sheer masonry.
Fingernails scrape the watertank.
The boys in plimsolls pogo on the parapet.

The village among brothers, the place I...

Glinchy

He'd peel a golfball with a penknife
he'd found on a river-strand
and cured with wire wool.

There'd be bets
the ball 'd not strip
in a oner,
and they'd be right –
golfballs are not oranges –
but the single white skin
was in Glinchy's hands
at the upshot.

'A hole in one.'

The inside was elastic
twined tight
like a statistic
for nylon
gripping the dwindling globe.
He'd pluck it to unreel it,
a kind of music,
test it in his arms' span,
then stretch it
road wide between lamp posts.

On the boulders of a rockery
we'd all sit back
waiting for the ambling car.

The elastic always snapped, but the driver
clocked the tension,
the line on the windscreen
tighten.

Glinchy'd say:
It wizny uz.

Elan

Brakes on the old new TR
a shoelace, snapped.
Dad steering the bends
on descending gears
(Ceylon, the packet of tea's
stepped precipices).

Or the alligator on the drive,
'The first Capri in Scotland – purple!'
pinks my brother's hands
in the driver's door.

Or, 'We're poorer, boys,'
and the red Elan
skulks on shabbier grit.

By the Escort's boot
Mum counts soup.

The Kirstys

Kirsty – that's a name
so Scottish, so
compelling.

The Kirstys I love,
and used to love (a swingpark
in that comfortable housing estate,
colours of their anoraks), the low
voices of Kirstys in their teens,
intimate as the flirts
my elder brothers were,
the fights, the neatness
of the jeans of Kirstys,
the lazy ache of too much –
the taste of her mouth is the taste
in the mouth – French kissing,
the scent of a girl
on your lambswool sweater
those miles after parting.

Kirsty, Kirsty, Kirsty.

Nick in the isotherm

Nearside, palmtrees,
a sea loch.

Higher in the hire car.
Above the anchorage, the lowest gear.
Purchase the hill.

In the wheelhouse of the motorcaravan,
before you, past you, a father, a mother.
At the rivetted glass a crew of children,
your own gaze, your own wave, holidays
in the metre between a motorhome
and a couple's car.

They will berth by the trees.

What made you?

Tarmac as hot as mouths.
The bypass, the bypassing.

My father's record collection

The hard black Corryvreckan
is static.
All the blues are quiet
in the white-washed attic.

There's a dead shining black,
a brittle hour.
Between Beethoven and Broadway
a pressed black flower.

Renfrewshire in Old Photographs

Reservoir

The river hasn't a legend to stand on –
if the trout could walk on water
they'd see the sea and long for it,
but there are no miracles
on a Council loch, BY ORDER.

It's a haw no a hazel
drappin its boz,
and fur wee manky fish.

No foolish maiden badly praying,
no bingo a Shannon –
your colonial Waverley
cuts no Congo.
Renfrewshire
is neither heart nor darkness.

There is the sound of water only.

Facts about trout

trout prefer
to stay underwater

the trout that can breathe
is a crocodile

there are two kinds of trout

one lives among mountains
the other in still water

farmed locally in large numbers
trout have important duties
abroad

trout are influential
at tables the world wide

trout never cry

they love the sky
for its flies

In spate

Specks of cream floating:
the river curdling.

A rope-swing touches water,
bridges' crotches go under,
second cars on credit
are tided over.
Antirrhinums – aquaflora.

At a sill a cup.
A fly, like a broken raven,
randomises
on the double glazing.

A hem of air
rises.

In the Parish of St Fillan

With his rucksack in the back
the hitchhiker brought you luck:
you drove the gorse-lined road
and the spikes didn't touch.
St Fillan and the stricken tree,
Warlock Road and the well of keys,
made you belong with them.

Three/four miles and his bonny talk
had done the missionary work:
he drove the gorse-lined road
and the fox was by the birch.
St Fillan and the stricken tree,
Warlock Road and the well of keys,
made you belong with them.

The fox was by the birch,
a mare by the hedge and curve:
he drove the gorse-lined road,
he made the living swerve.
St Fillan and the stricken tree,
Warlock Road and the well of keys,
made you belong with them.

The gain is in the grit.
The creatures knew the cut
granted by the gorse-lined road,
and the thorns did much.
St Fillan and the stricken tree,
Warlock Road and the well of keys,
made you belong with them.

Climb out the leafy wreck.
The driver is a rowan stick
planted by the gorse-lined road
and the saint inflamed the switch.
St Fillan and the stricken tree,
Warlock Road and the well of keys,
made you belong to them.

Dash

Smell the dash –
it's plastic with a clock
and a radio.

The singers are in their insides.
In the guitars, a throat of road.
My feet are articulate
and we have something
to lock in the boot.

As we are all the car –
the taste of the dust, the vinyl,
our shapes in the seats
(the speedo blinded
to the passenger side),

and tree, gantry, light, loch –

as we are all the car
stop the car.

Crash

Skew across the road
a tonne that's jumped the wingmirror,
car scrap in the sprung hawthorn.

In a pullover you have at the house
the driver's cut from the wreck.
She's walking – in the film of an accident.

Our doors still fit
but croak in their dents.
We're getting shut

to introduce ourselves.

Dry bed

A border, a marriage, a battle, a boy.
A river, a lip, a hook. A hook.

The loch drained, two blazed cars
reassert their shoulders,
half a land mile, facing.

On the shortest day the woolly sun
drives the family crate,
holed lamps light the coupé:
re-engined, bright.

A border, a marriage, a battle, a boy.
A river, a lip, a hook. A hook.

Hillman Avenger

When we raise a new cross on Barochan Hill
it will not be a Cross. To serve us instead
we'll haul up a wreck from Linwood's old works,
pull a car out a Renfrew scrappy.

Imagine the pulleys, the drive up the field,
the event. We'll rub its nose in its plinth, force
all its doors aghast. We'll build to last
that dive only ad cars pull themselves out of.

John Gallagher

Speak to me, John Gallagher
at work if no the house.
Ah've took up ma hem for you,
skooshed scent in ma blouse.

Ma says you're a boy fae the Port,
a druggie and no all there.
She minds your sensitive hands
were fists at the Kilma Fair.

Come to the shop, John Gallagher,
meet me on ma break.
If you're no a Prudential man
that's a risk Ah'll have to take.

Ghosts, Craigends House

Their spilling garden–party voice
brought me, startled, close.
I stopped before the orchard postern gate
and watched their dresses lift
and gather, show their knees.

Crouching out on ladders,
up beneath
fat Victoria plums
as firm and tight
as bruises on the cheek,
they plucked their father's fruit.

Inscription for the Manor Pool

Singing
you dropped me in the silver.

I wish I was the wisest fish,
the Golden Age's bubble-talker,
carpe diem, the fish of laughter.

I wish I was the privilege fish,
the gold who waits within the water –
who sees, who feels,
who knows the bathing daughter.

Deb to deb

You wasted an expensive invitation:
your gift, his
disappointment.

He'll say: 'Shot silk consumes you.'
You'll rustle.

He'll say: 'You're hollow.'
You'll empty yourself
with laughter.

He'll say: 'Your shoulders
are chicken
browned in fat.'
You'll admit
you were finished.

His lip.

Inscription for the Laverock Stone

The Laverock Stone's a mistle thrush
as fat as the grocery vans
in Mackie's Wood, in ferns and dew,
three hundred yards behind its hill.
The bird's alive a day or two
in autumn, given sunlight then.
A watcher who will wait until
the thrush's shape and shadows rush
to fill the flesh of that squat stone,
will see cold rock take life again
but find himself, too soon, alone.

Fifteen years

Fifteen years since I saw you,
and now you're on my mind.
You were in a raspberry row
lingering down the line.

A wedding on the telly
pulled the workers in.
You looked at me, I was royalty,
you were taken in.

A bus, a train, a taxi or two
packed me up for the season.
I never gave a thought to you
though you gave me every reason.

I moved on, went south,
tried to change my private future.
Where rats were creeping out
I'd pin my family's picture.

Dives, holes and flaking squats –
on any floor I'd be grateful.
I dodged the property courts,
told the police, 'I'm peaceful.'

I'm white-collar now, honest.
Are you still the farmer's daughter?
Free? In harness?
Have you fallen for a broker?

Ach, the tongue's the thing, the kiss,
what hopes get spoken.
What's sacred is only trust
and damned the promise broken.

Fifteen years since I saw you,
and now you're on my mind.
You were in a raspberry row
loitering down the line.

Quilted Leather

The Argument

There was no argument.
A man lived with a woman.
Their first large memory: a bank holiday.

Over the years they shared some clothes.
She wore an unfamiliar shirt.
He became suspicious.
He kept quiet.

She left him.
He saw her on to the train.
He had written a poem.
He sealed it in an envelope.
He kept it in his coat.
There was an intimate goodbye.
He left his coat behind.

He had bought a diary.
She looked in all the pockets.
She saw the envelope and the diary's receipt.

Piecing

Returned: letter and a receipt

If you are strapped for evidence.

If what cannot be believed
finds an inside pocket
with a receipt that you do remember,
corroborating. If you yourself
saw her on the sleeper,
coat on rack so you could hold her.

(On the bunk her handbag pants amends
with a bestseller and the weekend's
blanket of papers.)

If that was the leave-taking, steady;
lips, the martingales of goodbye.

Two shirts

Someone wore someone's shirt.

A woman wears the top of a man
and the motif is a cockerel.
I love this in general
(we shared a shirt called LABEL)
but the creature is home to roost.

The heart is a loose household glove, pinker
when full of hand, the comb of a cock.
The heart is a hankerchief in the pen pocket
of no one I know.

In the coat

A diary's receipt:
THANK YOU three ninety-nine THANK YOU
'Aye, might as well keep the evidence.'

What cannot: a verse-letter.

Warm air.

Describe me inaccurately I said

His goodbye

The letter he meant to fold in my arts page,
place in my presented clutch-bag perhaps.
Chickened out, but left it in his anorak.
An accident. Fear of woman with holdall.

(A man's shirt does not prove a man,
but he knew. I said to myself:
pick a door, leave the plunging old horse.)

Break

It is not right to forget, say,
the best bank holiday, pale bodies and not-exactly-blotches,
the bicker-raid, meaning no bickering,
meaning indecency prevailing after a harvest,
meaning the labourers snibbing their lunch-baskets,
meaning he really did read dictionaries.

Describe me inaccurately I said.

INSPRAICH: *The furniture of a horse.*
Charming.

KIR. *Cheerful, fond* (he hoped) *amorous.*
I was kir.

PELTIS HOYLL. *An opprobrious designation for a woman,*
equivalent perhaps to a tan-pit;
a hole for steeping pelts in.
Funny that, ha-ha. Empty the language bin
on yersel, y' geek.

He did.

CATRIDGE: *A diminutive man fond of women.*
Wants don't get, I said, and you're only small
where it counts.

MICHTIE: *Of high rank –*
Rank.
stately –
Some state I think.
strange, surprising, potent in the sense of liquor.
Licker or a po-tent? You, laddie, are a chancer.

CHANCY? *Fortunate, happy,*
promising good fortune,
conversant with the magical arts.
That seemed true.

Covering

Dear love, I enclose. I haven't opened
(can see the line breaks).
I cannot give address.
I cannot send anorak. Can
receipt, enc.

Scraps

I meant it as a letter. I meant it.
I made a word or two more tensile,
all English, tried to end it.

Everything must be unopened again.

Understand this: stand under the holed roof
of the tannery; the barndance of the cow-stumps.
In tannery town, dairy cows smile.

It's as if I was born left-handed,
taught 'right'; every written word a body lie.
Then we were airing our cotton on our sweat,
dancing like two left-handeds.

Two twirling cattle tore a door from their oblong.
The radar of the ceilidh was broken –
a tawse that had scarred us was a ribbon connecting us,
a loose ribbon connecting us,
begging our waists to use all the fresh grey air.

Recently, I've been low.

I travel with my wallet
pursing its lips in my pocket.

Gentians

in memory of my mother

The day before my mother's funeral

Tilt all your body in the lane's dash
and you're parallel with the rain.
The three brothers seem to know this:
ahead, they miss every drop.

We know our jackets again, heavy
as if someone else's, cloth wet through.
My hand in your hand
in your lined deep pocket.

Behind us my father holds his fishing
hat not tightly to his head and runs,
walks, and runs.

My mother's palette

We're getting thinner.

You pat your counterpane.
Your first oil,
blown sand abrasive,
hangs before you –
a diminished window.

Outside it,
the big-clad boys with their father
dig a baiting,
a sprung cockerel, furious, twitching,
crouches beneath a Dormobile.
Not miles away, an unSinhalese orchid
bows with spontaneous saliva.

I'm not eating enough
and should go back to meat.

Difficult sky

Orange pot mums, a choir at the table.
Brown bottles, like phosphate.
Pills, rare-seeded in foil.

We know, yet, our garden –
the frail blue gentians
are risen with us
back then.

A jigsaw of geraniums
and boats like the rooftops,
difficult sky,
buckle in my mother's lap.
We are working it out.

At ease

Scotland hits eighty in May.

An electric mower blows its nose.

The explaining murmur
is my father by the ladders;
the Macmillan visitor,
months into this
conversation,
is at ease.

With my shirt off, everything is ridiculous:
dad in shorts and people in the wrong places.
Inside, like church, when mum says garden
she means an English one.

The last kitchen

Turn to the taps and turn them on:
do you remember every sink
you've washed dishes in,
how home is in the time
the basin takes to fill,
the shape of the aluminium,
the kind of overflow?

Wash crocks here
and know those kitchens again.
Remember Mum singing
'Love is a many splendoured thing',
as Dad showed the drippers a cloth?

Later, you can read your future
in the scraps and froth
that vision's Corryvreckan
will leave you.

You will not
leave this kitchen
when you know it.

Tube Shelter Perspective

An image is a stop the mind makes between uncertainties
Djuna Barnes, *Nightwood*

We'd had a wager. The rodents snuffling
by the electric tracks – were they fat black mice
or starving rats? I put a Scottish note
on two sons of the plague, you a roundish pound
on Mickey and his spouse, and then all heard
a busker start with his sharp bone flute…

The animals stepped into their darkness.
As the train clapped in I noticed a boy
in tears before the underground's police
near the gates. He wore a brace on his leg.
The carriage doors opened and we crept on,

and then the screaming. It must have been him,
the boy I mean, while the busker began
to play much harder, 'Accompaniment
for Yell'. He filled the station, the tight skulls
of every one of us. Harmonising.

The doors shut up, the sounds not exactly,
but the train gripped and was through the portal,
the music and the voice simply away.
In darkness shot through with our light, I touched
your hand – and jolted! A child's smooth fingers!…

The whole carriage is a contented crèche,
and because I'm tall all the kids are thinking
I'm Sir. What will I tell them? And, much worse,
what of my now insistent conviction
that Milk and Honey, our destination,
is a trick station, closed before the war?

Through an exit a fireman with a concourse round him
steps back.
Our carriages don't
          coagulate.

Stop, and in a tunnel of radio
a probe is among moons.

Stop, and as if water refused to drown a body
the Dead Sea scrolls
                    live.

Before Christ was unwired,
rabbis frothed at variants:
look at the scraps as an unpicked quilt
from a village of embroiderers,
embellishment sung-in.
Pressed to sew just tack-stitch,
as news of the seamless sweatshirt ripped
through temples
they took their patches to the caves
like a lump in their throat.

In a crevice a white lizard cracks a gold beetle.
A see-through fish trembles its heart to swim.

Marella, Sidneya, Ogygopsis[1]
have been carved alive again:
new phyla in a torch's o!
Hallucigenia: seven mouths extending
from my torso, embarrassing
as red cross flags gabbing
at a trooping the colour,
saying the Royal Family and
the Institute of Contemporary Arts
are in cahoots –

    The heterodigetic analepsis
problematises temporality, decentralising
constructions of entity, power, capital and, paradoxically,
Aqua Libra, giftcards, and realpolitik.
The locus mapped, in unconclusion (and I use that word
advisedly), defines

– Mall-practice. (Lower vertebrates
aspire to be stone: shark and suckerfish
comprehend orts and good dentistry.)

1   The use of a footnote in a poem
implies the reader's ignorance
and the poet's inability
to master the poetic form.
Its rise, like that of free verse,
can be traced to the marginalisation of poetry
in an art free market
in which records, the novel and the broadcast media
have competed successfully.
Another factor has been
poets' envy of popularisers
of scientific discovery,
social history, and other information
susceptible to sentimental interpretation.

These names refer to fossils
in the Burgess Shale deposits
in B.C.

Paleontology is just
a boys' adventure:
in this man-hole
half the kinds of dinosaur
are females of the other half.

Stop. Shashi Kapoor stretches
from *Shakespeare Wallah* to *Sammy & Rosie*
and I mind the gap –
            from the tannery and the tawse
  to the jacket racks
  on the Mile End Road.

I depend from this handle's fist,
make like an essential strut.

At the next station
no detraining, too.

A bomb, or something civil?
Fishermen in oilskins wave us through
and we are a submarine:
the nets have no snags.

A jellyfish pants on an estuary's cement,
guts for brains –
threshed rhubarb in a badge of gelatin,
a trilobyte on a magnate's partied carpet,
cans on a string
mewling to a honeymoon cab.

if the harmonica is played with competence
by a victim of an industrial accident
I AM NOT HOMELESS I AM HUNGARY

if a cough behind a graphic designer
places a seed of saliva on his nape

if there is a cocker at velocity
brushing the conveyor-walkway

if

I am breathing the breath of a woman
I have known the breath of for eighteen months.
I am breathing the breath of a man
with an oatflake on the dent of his lip.
I am breathing the breath of a gourmand,
I am breathing the breath of
vocal common-sense.

If they breathe in all at once
my ticket will expire.

Vallejo,
someone with her nose-stud in your book
dunted me as she tried to get out
and I think I caught a translation.

Your transformer shrieks at my ankle!
Everyone's watches just sniff,
are trusting no one.
All the same, they still can't keep
their hands to theirselves.

I can hear the managers
guzzling a can –
just a meniscus in there
or an insole lipping the lip.

How come the snack
chooses the wrong spit?

How come I'm conducting this
with everyone else's lightning?

On the tannoy I can hear
the muezzin singing
to Whitechapel's underground gallery.

Crosses have been crissed.

Upstairs the District Line's delays
percolate in a golden minaret.

I'll tell you what's been on my mind. I've
given in to what the train means. I've
given out too many starts. The stops
were just fools' stops: as if I had a
seat and offered it up to the man
who's growing out of that scratched crutch
by the doors: just as he eyed yes I thought,
'It's a favour!' That kept him standing.

With Balham Station I want to be banal,
call it Balaam and think of the Angel,
call it bedlam and think of Royal Oak.
But I'm escaping names – Bank's accretions.
You know the deeds committed with titles –
naming oil-rigs with a Piper or a Thistle,
a company's chuckle at symbols owning owners,
podgy helicopters lugging from rig to rig
like clegs at candle-lit tables.

Rigs. Who's been rigging
this specimen cheque's
Anytown –
where the owners are squatters
(the squatters, owners)?

Don't think platforms
(oil or Underground)
float like ships
on the greasy waters
beneath tower and town.
Get beneath the name.

In the Blitz a bomb bursts a watermain,
and sixty drown in Balham Station.

Wipe the tears for ever from their eyes
but remember.

A lorry with windscreen grills
and black fruit on its back
is lifted by a team of women
towards a moving walkway.
Before they release it
they say, 'Driver,
tell every aperture on the surface
we know they will treat you
as if you were honest,
that they'll honour you
and call us the enemy within.'

Tell them
the middle names of our girls:
Frances, Comrie.

Tell them
meadows and water,
Seafield and Killoch,
are the underworld's seizures.

Tell them
Icarus is not unknown to us:
Longannet, Solsgirth.

Tell them
the difference
between Tweedledee
and Polmaise and Polkemmet.

Tell them we know
what power is:
Castlehill, Monkton Hall,
Castlebridge, Barony.

The long-closed stations –
what good's their past to me now?
What's in there? Grubby copes,
a bricked-up exit,
an echo that still can't
lie still.

To tell the truth
I'm the same for the echo
and that echo
tunnelling in my heart.

Brickwork in daylight,
ferns in the mortar.
Glimpses of men
and a crane in a crater.

Cables on a trellis,
bolts in the gravel.
Grass on a ledge
and the wire of a bramble.

A beggar with manners –
how accommodating.

The skull's a casing.
Look at a gasket –
it's an inkblot
and now you're making connections.

Inside the sealed unit
an engine block swivels
on the elbow of a pair of calipers,
body implied.

Paolozzi, you're underground
and as popular
as public transport.

Work-tired in a few stations
the head almost
ratchets down to a slump.

I'm a grubby bird
sleeping on the wing.

Even at the stops
I don't start.

It's as if we were nudging the carpet with our shoes,
the red registry office like a joke on everyone else,
and later, as if we forced the guests to eat no meat,
as if we found an Underground carriage tidy and empty,
or a ghost station from Ramsay MacDonald's England,
and I promised exclusively it was 'British Museum',
the black tiles artefacts for all,
but ours only, the compartment, the stairway off.

Two years and not a dance between us.
Now, we're children within the rotors
of a skipping rope.

Other guests stop their chat.
Or we are at home and realise something:
we share an Underground compartment
without noticing, and that's
almost how we met.

Foals of the Foals

With is

To ravel with you in ripening light.
To worry and adore the stacking cups of your spine.

What I come with
is a dubious country,
a prejudice against people like us,
nationals who've dropped to couples,
two martens agog
under a tired Scots pine.

Our table is empty,
a summer curling pond.
Come on out on the town!
I've the night-bus map
you leant me
when I was only a Scot.

Stopper

At the front of the top deck
we're some kind of couple.

Through the smear
a harmonica's bad teeth
smile on a shelter's roof.
A woman leans
to keep her Alsatian.
All solicitors keep cactuses
in teapots.

No, lean your way.
Touch my sleeve
if you see anything I miss.

Saying the swim

I am in the two of us at the breast stroke,
our hair flat, black, painted,
your eyes darker and larger, shining,
and the pool is not now municipool
the sink and the Atlantic –
and swallowing and breathing are shuffling
the air between the banknotes in our leather lungs –
you look and choke, tread water, glisten,

you are in the two of us at the crawl,
our heads down, blundering, shaking
a sheet of water, a duvet between us,
snapping up the air,
a bedcover patterned with swimming,
and the two of us folding ourselves over,
sinking and slightly rolling, coming up, all out,
under, sinking and rolling,

the two of us in the two of us,
swimming.

Taking hand

You found the time
to photocopy your hands,
the matt walls of the camera a bath,
a speck on the glass spinning you
on its splinter, internal mail
unfolding at a wedding
beginning in a multi-storey.
Chuffed as car doors and then civil,
'The meeting's quorate, love,'
a little do about touch, red–eye,
and the music stand a sapling in winter,
fuzzbox and flanger, sheet music later,
a song we know now and feedback.

The wedding rings

What they say and the gold itself:
not so much embracing, embracing us,
as being their own circles, clinkered from

a sovereign and a Renfrewshire nugget.
Inside, ions like mines five-jack up
in a wave's midrise,

froth themselves in charge –
all so tense they just shine.

At length

'Can I hear discussions?'

The Midnight Money Report
loans you forty winks,
long wave and sleep at length,
tall to pillows.

The strain is off your cartilage.
Against a basket of currencies,
breath.

You're in the black.

Sense and a minor fever

Curtains breathing, books not clapping,
drying clothes surround us.
I can hear an overtaking,
the grind of a train of heaps,

and here's you, sleeping,
irritable, sifting the air
as if a hair
at the back of your tongue
knew something,

as if your lungs were listening to me
with your heart's healthy scepticism.

Doodlebug

Your daughter trims the jib
of our open window.

A walking stick taped
to a plane tree frets.

Like a spinnaker,
the two storeys of your bus
lift,
travel the distance
between two kerbs.

No one is killed:
there is a death in a terrace.
Where there is precision,
many.

The street is footling twigs
and green leaves to ankle height.

A flimsy factory turning gyroscopes
keeps
perfect
balance.

The men leave their dies
and begin sweeping.

Singer

My mother's father, just a father,
lifts a toolkit of field mushrooms,
gills turbines. Flopped patches
are heaped in the muddied sewing basket.
That whole sloppy meadow
is a family appliqué, an engine in section.

It is six thirty: a machined morning.
A Messerschmidt, crew as ready
for home, tacks a hem of bullets
just past his strawy boots.

Foals of the foals

A husky will overheat in a cellar.
A Przewalski horse is stocky,
bad-tempered and confined.

A 'handicap' is your brother,
nine or ten, still in nappies,
in your arms, in your reins.

This means: the girl in the duffel
by her dad's woven fence,
laughing, is you,

and like that look just now
that laugh is not remembering.
All that

is not cleared up,
but the vet's
one-minute visit
and your ice-pup
ran riot
in the snow-filled yard.

The foals of the foals
in your bedside book, too,
have their wildness
in the wilderness now,
're-introductions',

and, once in a while,
John sups half a pint
in the Fox and Hounds.

The battle of the horses

The thoroughbreds, tiaras for teeth,
dab their corners with white flags –
talk common sense, wait for sweet.

On our sill: a stallion and a mare.
They break their glaze, smile.
Muscular clay nudges blinkers.

The battle of the horses,
between laughters.
Sweating horses
on the gristle round the heart.

At a Mary

At a nunnery with dishcloths
the tat-racks have our minutes.

Drizzle.

Up the smudged hill, a Mary,
praying or diving. Being white.

Tablet-slabby the path, not a path
a stream. Rhododendrons

dripping not sniffing.

Fluff-warm in our layers of wool,
in our blue cagoules; breathing that.

The rocks are giant steps, juds,
gravel's on the flags.

The seeping,

the wet woody light, the leggy shrubs.
We're you and I, pushing the slope

up the slope – into the open,
the tumbling grass, the slapped rocks.

Gusts.

All the hills are with us
there and there, and higher.

We are Nature Lovers; think highly.
Within her railings, streaky Mary

is drenched.

We're stepping up, taking the plinth.
Two black goats

can't finish their mouthfuls.
Scare /dismissal?

Hefty and gone.

Love charm of Cong, Co. Mayo

He's a quiet man
that mouse,
that cat, that
animal-of-unclear-genus,
squirrel-of-no-tail,
lynx-with-round-ears,
that crouching deer.

She's quiet
that horse,
that saddle-bags beast,
that worker dog,
jewelled wolf,
stag-with-no-horns, marten,
that badger blanketed in bronze.

We're tight-lipped, too,
the two of us,
and hope that folk
make neither
head nor tail of us –
so you've a home here,
holiday-thing,
on our windowsill
or on the bookcase –
that is,
if you'll keep the peace,
and keep us guessing,
and keep us.

The Giant

The Giant

Your first written message – a postcard, the Giant,
the rude Rude Man of quaint Cerne Abbas –
a long weekend with your parents –
cream teas, a cramped tea-room –
chairs that scrape the tiles.

'Where's his shorts?' your mother's chuckling,
'I knew friends got diseases from Thameside jaunts.'

Sometimes you can't see the light in people's eyes
but you know the light.

*

Your first written message,
cheeky, cheerful, cherished here –

'You risk… Englishness.' I take
all the claptrap back,

the state identity me me me.
I scrap the abstract, the years

neck-deep in, neck-deep in. I take
almost all the claptrap back.

*

Your note a taper, you'd started
to burn me clean –

amorous candlelight
and real marks of combustion

in this distant here,
this fifteen years here,
this two-lives-started-,
late-, later here.

99

Your card not a gift, a gift-tag.
Our old life the present.

*

Sometimes you can't see the light in someone's eyes
but you know the light.

*

No one should act
as if love was resistance to enthusiasm,
one thing, one thing, one thing –
one thing, one thing –
as if love was agreeing
to reasonable expectations,
acceptance of a single species of love,
affection in monoculture,
passionate kisses for the coat hanger, the word 'love'.

I mean myself.

*

Forgiveness tries to free us,
brings us close.

*

No one thinks love
is Cerne Abbas as a naturist,
love as Cerne Abbas and Cerne Abbas as satire
(it's now thought Cerne Abbas was a satire –
on Cromwell) –

Thug-King God-Cromwell
slaughtering your Irish ancestors.
Club-Prick Bomber-Cromwell
slaughtering my English ancestors.

Love can't be
the word 'slaughtering',
centuries-long, repeated to a faction.

*

A chirpy postcard ('The First English Nudist') –

count a year or ten, a snoring evening, hand-in-weary-hand –
we're collapsed before the fireplace (blocked off).

The children, content around us, absorbed,
pretend to write.

Sometimes you can see, sometimes you can see
the light – in a person's eyes – and you don't know that light.

*

Final goodbyes, all the risks and anxieties of a life,
dogs unmuzzled, owls on the last oak –
suited street sellers hawking the smallest kite in the world.

This lifetime's ladlit – please ditch this script
at the dentist's, with *Practical Yachting*,
Macho and *Goodbye.*

No time now for share and share alike,
madrigals in the zesty juice-bar, coughs, viscous waves,
Orchestre Baobab, nailed down windows
a claw-hammer cannot release.

And no hope of seeing you, more than a sister,
without hurt.

Final goodbyes, all the risks and anxieties of love.
No hope now (all the no's, all the now's)
for a better misunderstanding,
the thousand species once supported by a single oak,
a world created by a bright tattoo on a giant's back.

You see the light in someone's eyes
and you know that light.

Texts

Texts jolt,
accrue –

            fragments only,
            'The Truth about True'.

Gifts… Children…
one or two?

            Urgent… poetry?
            Backlit, blue.

Marriage and honey,
texts laden, about to drip.

            Some words I grasp.
            Some… elude my grip.

When the animals are freed

After she says I don't love you,
I could kill you, how
dare you – speak to me like that,

after I've said 'Oh,'
and 'Oh,' and
'Oh, I see,'

after we
are still speaking at least,
I'm permitted to read,

I'm desired to read,
I'm authorised to read, Daddy.

After bathless bath time
is a defeat –
I read.

Noah's Ark: retold.

When the animals are freed
she holds my hand.
She falls not quite asleep.

A traditional activity

the paper chain

a paper father
paper twins

rip

weight the plane
with a paper-clip

*

the paper-chain

a paper mother
paper twins

rip

tiara / swan /
ocean-going ship

Small dense hours

Music to sleep.

Do you... still listen to discussions?
A little paper-yellow light and you're fine-tuning,
a child again with pocket torch,
secret vitamins (raisins), a sponsored read.

Darkness can be held with a wedge of radio.
Darkness can dissolve if you can dissolve
in art appreciation, civil debate.

Will you remember, last night was it,
'The Need for Faith' made you, finally,
thankfully, neither here nor there?

I almost pray for us to sleep corrected, to breathe
synchronised, complementary breaths,
miles peacefully apart.

Music to sleep. No, the song's over and I
still can't lie still. When will the flat-out flickers
call the small dense hours a day,
click themselves, me, gently off?

Music.

Duchal Wood

I'm back, and the air's around me,
lungs in the pink again.
A sense of the height of the beeches,
the pines, the birches,
millions of years in their company
but fresh when the breeze is flirting.

The ground holds everything
so my footprints are my memory,
no lookbacks though, just following –
finding my path find its falling.

Hollytrees claw
darkness into their leaves,
their burden.
Reddish ragged robins
in the uncleared clearing
make light of their ribbons.
I know the pale undersides
of the leaves of wild raspberries,
the tough but flowering
tumbles of bramble,
how fungus is wood
but also leather,
how nettles don't tremble
except together, a tactic.

I know the long chassis,
its cab all twisted
on its stiffened shoulder,
the ground just glass
in the state of powder,
the tyres now minerals,
and the homeless or hearty
a witness – of diminishing ash.

Open the paper window

Open the paper window

Open the paper window –
there's whisky of course, repatriated from duty-free.

A little ankle bracelet –
Mhairi where are you now?

A crouching platoon, months under the double bed,
a lick-down mine.

Open the paper window – snow! (the only white Christmas) –
four brothers, wool bales, piled low on the hurtling sledge.

Scaletrix. A red car, a green car –
they're from my father to my father.
We were just intermediaries.

It seems repetitive to mention the train set,
but later you could hide hash in the papier-mâché tunnel.

Open the window. It counts against me
I can remember not a single present my mother received.

Open the window – a bit of peace and quiet from you shower
or there'll be no Christmas this year!

Open the window – a tangerine,
miraculous, the orange for learners.

A tall candle, E-type red, has melted the pewter candlestick.

There's a brown-and-green black-and-white tv,
call it television please.

Bells and mirrors for a baby thirty-five years ago.

Bells and mirrors for a baby ten years ago.

Thomas Hardy, cheer us up!

Open the paper window –
Mum and Dad are going to Midnight Mass.
(You're in trouble – you were seen enjoying yourself
at Midnight Mass.)

How *does* Father Christmas fill the stocking?
We stayed awake as long as we could!

Open the window –
glowing pastels.

Open the window –
tinsel.

Open the window.
Try not to electrocute yourself this time! They aren't sweeties!

Black bags of exhausted wrapping.
She definitely said batteries included.

For the nineteenth bloody time you're not getting a gun
for Christmas!

Open the window.
Too much brandy butter.

Open the window, the last paper window
(it's quiet here, under the tree) –

the present: abstract, perfect,
waiting to be opened.